Faith Under Fire

Church Times Study Guide

Faith Under Fire

Exploring 1 Peter and Revelation

John Holdsworth

CANTERBURY PRESS
Norwich

© John Holdsworth 2006

First published in 2006 by the Canterbury Press Norwich
(a publishing imprint of Hymns Ancient &
Modern Limited, a registered charity)
St Mary's Works, St Mary's Plain,
Norwich, Norfolk, NR3 3BH

www.scm-canterburypress.co.uk

All rights reserved. No part of this publication may be reproduced,
stored in a retrieval system, or transmitted, in any form or
by any means, electronic, mechanical, photocopying or
otherwise, without the prior permission of
the publisher, Canterbury Press

Scripture quotations are from the Revised Standard Version of the
Bible, copyright 1946, 1952 and 1971 by the Division of Christian
Education of the National Council of the Churches of Christ in the
USA. Used by permission. All rights reserved.

British Library Cataloguing in Publication data

A catalogue record for this book is available
from the British Library

ISBN 1-85311-659-9
978-185311-659-9

Typeset by Regent Typesetting, London
Printed and bound by
Gallpen Colour Print, Norwich

Contents

Introduction vii

1 Christians Under Fire 1
2 Worshipping Despite it All 12
3 Why Worship When You're Suffering? 20
4 What to Do Next 23

Introduction

Worship and suffering – getting the feel of 1 Peter and Revelation

1 Peter and Revelation are not generally studied together. If you study them separately, 1 Peter is a great place to start exploring the New Testament letters because few, if any, of the traditional critical questions are resolved. So the study is not just about learning other people's answers to questions, but about recognizing how the critical problems are related to each other, and trying out your hand as a critic, knowing that your results will probably be at least as credible as anyone else's. There is, for example, no general agreement about when 1 Peter was written, why it was written, where it was written from, or who wrote it. There are varying views on whether its main thrust is suffering, with incidental references to worship; or whether its main thrust is worship, with incidental references to suffering; or whether actually it's about how to live a Christian life. In which case there is disagreement about whether it's urging its readers (whoever they are) to be counter-cultural or not. Just as with an Australian TV soap, if you haven't read a book on 1 Peter for some time, it's relatively easy to pick up the critical plot by reading one that was written more recently.

The same thing is not true of Revelation. Here, the last 25 years or so have seen striking developments in critical appreciation. This can be either stimulating or off-putting to the new casual student, who finds difficulty sometimes, perhaps, identifying a foothold from which to scale this majestic NT peak. And this is a shame because in my experience at least, everyone wants to understand Revelation. Start a Bible study group, especially with young people, and ask them what they want to study – and see if I'm right. Obviously, no booklet this length can do justice to all the developments in thinking about Revelation, but we shall be writing from a perspective that is aware of them.

What this study aims to do is to acquaint you with aspects of the current state of scholarship on these two books, and so to encourage you to read them with fresh eyes; but not attempting to do so by simply listing what's happened in the academic world. Rather I want us to approach the books in the search for an answer to a problem that affects all Christians to this day, and to allow that search to tell us what we need to know about scholarship. The problem is: what is the relationship between worship and suffering? And the reason these books can help us is that of all the books of the New Testament outside the Gospels at least, in relation to their length, they have the most to say about suffering, and the most references to worship. Moreover, it is possible to hold a view, with critical integrity, which says that these books were directed to roughly the same geographical area at roughly the same time as each other – in other words, some aspects of their context may be similar.

It is interesting, though not often remarked upon, that the books which do have the most references to suffering also have the most references to worship. This immediately raises a number of big questions:

- Why should that be?
- Does that give us any clues as to how the early churches dealt with suffering, or how they understood worship?
- Does it help us to see how worship developed?
- Is it the case that suffering people understand worship most fully?
- Is worship, as the NT understands it, really possible in a culture of wealth, prosperity and plenty?

By the end of the study, then, you should have some more biblical tools with which to tackle those awesome questions, as well as a greater understanding of the critical state of play on 1 Peter and Revelation.

The way we shall approach this is as follows. Section 1 will look at suffering in 1 Peter and Revelation. Section 2 will look at worship in 1 Peter and Revelation. Section 3 will look at some options for the reader in making sense of this material and relating it to the work of scholars, and to our own experience. There will be a short final section about resourcing for those who want to dig deeper.

1
Christians Under Fire

How do these two books describe suffering?

1 Peter

There are references to suffering scattered throughout 1 Peter. It is possible that there is a change of emphasis after 4.11. The references before then appear to speak about suffering in a general way, whereas after 4.11 they might be thought more urgent and contemporary.

> ### Exercise
> Read 1 Peter: 1.6, 7; 2.20; 3.14–17:
>
> In this you rejoice, though now for a little while you may have to suffer various trials, so that the genuineness of your faith, more precious than gold which though perishable is tested by fire, may redound to praise and glory at the revelation of Jesus Christ. . . . For what credit is it, if when you do wrong and are beaten for it you take it patiently? But if when you do right and suffer for it you take it patiently, you have God's approval. . . . But even if you do suffer for righteousness' sake, you will be blessed. Have no fear of them, nor be troubled, but in your hearts reverence Christ as Lord. Always be prepared to make a defence to any one who calls you to account for the hope that is in you, yet do it with gentleness and reverence; and keep your conscience clear, so that, when you are abused, those who revile your good behaviour in Christ may be put to shame. For it is better to suffer for doing right, if that should be God's will, than for doing wrong.

> *Now read 4.12, 14, 19; and 5. 8–10:*
>
> Beloved, do not be surprised at the fiery ordeal which comes upon you to prove you, as though something strange were happening to you. . . . If you are reproached for the name of Christ, you are blessed, because the spirit of glory and of God rests upon you. . . . Therefore let those who suffer according to God's will do right and entrust their souls to a faithful Creator. . . . Be sober, be watchful. Your adversary the devil prowls around like a roaring lion, seeking some one to devour. Resist him, firm in your faith, knowing that the same experience of suffering is required of your brotherhood throughout the world. And after you have suffered a little while, the God of all grace, who has called you to his eternal glory in Christ, will himself restore, establish, and strengthen you.
>
> Do you think this shows that some sudden dramatic event has overtaken the writer, or that he is just developing his argument with more specific examples?

In addition to the descriptions of Christians' suffering there are notable references to Christ's suffering as well. 1.19 draws on the imagery of the sacrificial lamb; 2.21–4 describes the sufferings of Christ's trial and crucifixion using language that is found in the New Testament only here and in the Gospel accounts of the Passion. 3.18 and 19 is a very strange passage, which has several things to say about Christ suffering. 4.1 and 4.13 are further references.

Connected problems

So what does all this add up to? There are three main possibilities:

- the references could be to some state-sponsored persecution;
- they could be a response to a kind of harassment of Christians by their neighbours at a local level, which though serious on occasion falls short of persecution as such;

- the language and rhetoric of suffering might be being used to describe a situation in which physical suffering is not being experienced as such, but in which there is disappointment at the slow progress of the Christian gospel.

In 1 Peter, one critical problem is always connected with lots of others, and nothing is ever as straightforward as it seems. If we want to relate the book to some known period of persecution then these are the problems we encounter:

- We're not sure when the book was written, or if it was written all at once (as our exercise above demonstrates). Various possibilities have been suggested which range from the early 60s, around the time of writing the first Gospel, to the time around 112 CE in the reign of the Emperor Trajan.
- There is some doubt as to how many periods of state persecution towards Christians there were during this time. There was (almost) certainly one, but possibly two, or three.

Arguments relating to either of these are sometimes muddied by a second agenda. For some people it is very important to establish that Peter the apostle wrote the letter. After all it is called 1 Peter and purports to be written by him. Actually that's not the big deal it would be nowadays. If I wrote a book about king Solomon and called it *The Half Blood Prince and the Doomed Temple* by J. K. Rowling, it would indeed be a scandal, but in New Testament times there were different conventions. If Peter were to be the author, the book would have to have been written before his death in the mid-60s – hence the urgency in the minds of some to establish this date in relation to other data such as known persecutions.

There are other problems about Peter being the author. In other parts of the New Testament Peter is portrayed as an ordinary bloke without literary accomplishment, but this letter is written in some of the best Greek in the New Testament. Perhaps he had a ghost writer, like some modern sportsperson having a newspaper column written for them because they couldn't write it with the same skill themselves (to put it as kindly as the libel laws will allow). Some people believe that Silas/Sylvanus acted in this way (see 5.12). Others think that this reference was a clever way of associating the author with Paul, whom we see accompanying Silas/Sylvanus in Acts chapters 15–18, 2 Corinthians 1.19, and 1 Thessalonians 1.1; and who delivers a letter at Acts 15.22. Another problem for early dating is that the ideas in 1 Peter are said to be more like other writings from later in the century. Nevertheless Peter could be the author, but actually, from the point of view of understanding what it all means today, it really doesn't matter who wrote it.

> ### Reflection
> When you read the Bible how important is it for you to know who wrote what you are reading? What kind of difference does it make? What kind of challenge is it to discover that Peter may not have been the author this book? What is at stake for you here?

Historical persecutions

For the most part, attempts at dating the book have relied on identifying the persecutions, so what are the options there for us?

The first systematic persecution of Christians by the state is attributed to **Nero** (emperor 54–68). He became emperor at the age of 17 in 54 CE and thereafter was responsible for many murders including those of several members of his own family. According to the ancient historian Suetonius he was universally hated and indulged in every kind of foul excess. In 64 there was a great fire in Rome which Suetonius quite openly accuses Nero of starting. Another historian, Tacitus, tells how Nero put the blame on Christians. These are described in the account as 'a class of men loathed for their vices' who hated the human race. They were killed either by being covered with the skins of wild beasts and being torn apart by dogs, or they were fastened to crosses, and when daylight failed were burned to serve as lamps. No one else describes these events in this way, though Suetonius alludes to it. The 60s were a very brutal period, culminating in the Jewish revolt and the destruction of the Jewish Temple. A later historian, Eusebius, writes of this time: 'Everywhere the people of the (Jewish) nation were pitifully destroyed as if they were foes.'

The emperor **Domitian** (emperor 81–96) was long thought to have instigated a period of persecution in the mid-90s. The evidence for this is largely circular, and based on the bloody descriptions of warfare in the book of Revelation, almost certainly written around that time. The problem is that based on the assumption of persecution, the Revelation passages are then read as if that assumption were fact. The only solid evidence of action against any Christian at that time is the banishment of the author of Revelation, John, to the island of Patmos (which doesn't really compare with being torn apart by dogs).

The emperor **Trajan** (emperor 98–117), while not an active persecutor of Christians, has left us a brief correspondence, showing how Christians were treated in this part of Asia around the year 112. Those accused were subject to a process of law, with the opportunity to recant. If they failed to do this they were executed. Being a Christian was thus understood to be a crime deserving death. Those who favour a late date for 1 Peter usually do so on the conviction that these kinds of circumstance best fit the descriptions of suffering in the book.

Reflection and Exercise

Read again 1 Peter 4.12 to the end:

> Beloved, do not be surprised at the fiery ordeal which comes upon you to prove you, as though something strange were happening to you. But rejoice in so far as you share Christ's sufferings, that you may also rejoice and be glad when his glory is revealed. If you are reproached for the name of Christ, you are blessed, because the spirit of glory and of God rests upon you. But let none of you suffer as a murderer, or a thief, or a wrongdoer, or a mischief-maker; yet if one suffers as a Christian, let him not be ashamed, but under that name let him glorify God. For the time has come for judgment to begin with the household of God; and if it begins with us, what will be the end of those who do not obey the gospel of God? And
> 'If the righteous man is scarcely saved,
> where will the impious and sinner appear?'
> Therefore let those who suffer according to God's will do right and entrust their souls to a faithful Creator.

> Do any of these scenarios seem to match?
>
> *Read also 3.13–17, in conjunction with 4.14:*
>
> > Now who is there to harm you if you are zealous for what is right? But even if you do suffer for righteousness' sake, you will be blessed. Have no fear of them, nor be troubled, but in your hearts reverence Christ as Lord. Always be prepared to make a defence to any one who calls you to account for the hope that is in you, yet do it with gentleness and reverence; and keep your conscience clear, so that, when you are abused, those who revile your good behaviour in Christ may be put to shame. For it is better to suffer for doing right, if that should be God's will, than for doing wrong. . . . If you are reproached for the name of Christ, you are blessed, because the spirit of glory and of God rests upon you.
>
> Does that change things for you? Look again at the account of Nero's persecution above. Are there any modern parallels that come to mind to the kind of cruelty that can imprint itself so vividly on the communal imagination?

Symbolic sufferings

A further possibility is that the author is using this very vivid language as a dramatic way of describing the progress of the Christian gospel, and particularly of describing setbacks and disappointments. In other words, perhaps it shouldn't be taken literally. The addressees are described as aliens and exiles. Both those terms could have a literal or a symbolic value. They may also refer to a particular social class of transient workers. They may even hark back to the Old Testament time of Exile to revive a symbol that still had resonance – the author says he writes from Babylon (5.13). In the same way it may be that the suffering is some kind of metaphor for the writer's understanding of the struggle between the power of the gospel and powers alien to it. There is a way of writing – described as 'apocalyptic' – also used by the author of Revelation which does use the language of suffering in this way as a means of coming to terms with the gap between faith and experience. On the one hand the gospel proclaims a mighty victory for God. On the other, experience shows Christians as powerless pawns, subject to a variety of sometimes malign authorities, all related to the seemingly insuperable power of Rome. Apocalyptic writing at this time is an attempt to bridge this credibility gap, and 1 Peter may be an example of it. This possibility and the alternatives are not mutually exclusive. The sufferings could be actual, as well as being used by the author as a symbol of the greater universal and even cosmic significance of what is happening.

Suffering and Revelation

Suffering in Revelation is more difficult to describe. However, this difficulty is not related to the dating of the book, which most commentators conclude is in the mid-90s. Revelation is not written as a single letter. An introduction is followed by seven letters to churches in the same part of Asia as 1 Peter – an area now part of western Turkey. In contrast to 1 Peter, there are no reflections on suffering as such here, and few descriptions of actual suffering in the Church. Indeed the book begins by telling us that it will describe 'what must soon take place' (1.1). John has been exiled to the island of Patmos. There is a reference to future imprisonment in the letter to Smyrna (2.10) and Antipas has been put to death in Pergamum (2.13), but that's about it. After this introduction, the writer adopts an apocalyptic style that presents cycles of visions and auditions leading to a climax in which faith is vindicated against all the odds and those who practised either immorality or idolatry are punished. What is undeniable is that there is an ethos of brutality about this book. It has the feel of a book written by and to people who know what suffering means and could mean. It might be that it was written at a time when memories of Nero's persecution are still fresh in the folk memory, but when there is little immediate persecuting activity. Indeed, perversely as it may seem, at least one commentator thinks the ideal context for the book is one of relative calm in which the writer wants to shake readers out of their complacency and apathy by reminding them of the bloody past, and urging them to treat the present as a time of significance.

> ### Reflection
>
> Think of the ways that the Nazi Holocaust has become a way of talking about and measuring suffering nowadays in Western culture, even though it happened 60 years ago. Think of the ways in which the freshness of this image is maintained. Now imagine if Nero's persecution had this effect on Christians. How might you expect to see that reflected in writings of this period?

Suffering in Revelation is certainly related to the power of the state. The book is very much about power and powerlessness, and about what empowers. It is also about appearance and reality. Rome appears great but is fatally flawed by her own corruption and is therefore weak. Christians appear weak but actually, in terms of universal destiny, the victory is theirs. Despite the otherworldly setting of some of the visions, there is a chilling imaginable earthiness to the carnage and disaster described, much of it related to the downfall of those apparently invincible institutions of what we might now call the military industrial complex.

> ### Exercise
>
> *Read Revelation chapter 18 with this in mind.* Note the brutal language and note also the details that give some insight into what are considered the symptoms of evil in this society – note especially for example the list in verse 13.

Some social and religious contexts

If we do assume that the context of both books is something other than outright state persecution, but rather something more localized and sporadic, it might be useful to reflect on what the social contexts were that put Christians at odds with their neighbours, and the religious contexts that prompted them to use the language of suffering and brutality so freely. Just a few pointers might give a sense of the problems.

- The area as a whole was enjoying disproportionate prosperity and unusual peace as a result of Roman rule. Anything which seemed at odds with this sense of gratitude was suspect. Christians would not accept that the state could take the place of God.
- There was civic pride on a massive scale and in places this may have resulted in a version of the emperor cult, or more likely a kind of gratitude for all that Rome represented, expressed in religious terms. Christians would have viewed this as a rival to the worship of the one God.
- Asia was a great place for belonging, with lots of civic guilds and societies essential for doing business and social location. Thyatira was a special centre for this, and in fact Christianity died out there fairly early. Many of these guilds would have been associated with pagan cults and ceremonies – anathema to Christians, who were then excluded.
- Some of the great cities had been traditional centres of worship for pagan deities such as the god of healing in Pergamum and the goddess Diana in Ephesus. These still helped give these places some identity. Their worship was tolerated by Rome, and in some cases was a local moneyspinner (see Acts 19.23 – the end, for an example of how Paul and his colleagues caused a real rumpus by threatening the tourist trade in Ephesus). Christians believed that only God could heal, and that pagan gods were powerless and socially dangerous, so believers were opposed.
- The area was prone to earthquakes and famines. Christians who didn't belong and didn't conform were obvious scapegoats in answer to the question: how could the gods let this happen?
- It may be that in any case Christians belonged to the lower and very vulnerable social class of 'resident aliens'. That is how they are described in 1 Peter (using a Greek word from which is derived the English word 'parish'). We might then compare them with foreigners in our own country, with work permits.
- Christians could expect no favours from Jewish communities. These communities also felt vulnerable and were afraid of losing privileges they had gained in the Roman empire, by being confused with Christians.

Exercise

Read Revelation 2.1–7 and 18–29:

'To the angel of the church in Ephesus write: "The words of him who holds the seven stars in his right hand, who walks among the seven golden lampstands.

'"I know your works, your toil and your patient endurance, and how you cannot bear evil men but have tested those who call themselves apostles but are not, and found them to be false; I know you are enduring patiently and bearing up for my name's sake, and you have not grown weary. But I have this against you, that you have abandoned the love you had at first. Remember then from what you have fallen, repent and do the works you did at first. If not, I will come to you and remove your lampstand from its place, unless you repent. Yet this you have, you hate the works of the Nicolaitans, which I also hate. He who has an ear, let him ear what the Spirit says to the churches. To him who conquers I will grant to eat of the tree of life, which is in the paradise of God." . . .

'And to the angel of the church in Thyatira write: "The words of the Son of God, who has eyes like a flame of fire, and whose feet are like burnished bronze.

'"I know your works, your love and faith and service and patient endurance, and that your latter works exceed the first. But I have this against you, that you tolerate the woman Jezebel, who calls herself a prophetess and is teaching and beguiling my servants to practise immorality and to eat food sacrificed to idols. I gave her time to repent, but she refuses to repent of her immorality. Behold, I will throw her on a sickbed, and those who commit adultery with her I will throw into great tribulation, unless they repent of her doings; and I will strike her children dead. And all the churches shall know that I am he who searches mind and heart, and I will give each of you as your works deserve. But to the rest of you in Thyatira, who do not hold this teaching, who have not learned what some call the deep things of Satan, to you I say, I do not lay upon you any other burden; only hold fast what you have, until I come. He who conquers and who keeps my works until the end, I

> will give him power over the nations, and he shall rule them with a rod of iron, as when earthen pots are broken in pieces, even as I myself have received power from my Father; and I will give him the morning star. He who has an ear, let him hear what the Spirit says to the churches."'
>
> Can you begin to put together a picture of life in these churches?

There are two religious contexts that are relevant:

- The one already mentioned of powerless people whose faith was at odds with their experience. They had to be convinced that the gospel was true and that this was a time of great significance in the history of the world. Within that history they had to feel that they occupied a special place, but suffering was somehow a prerequisite of the short interim between their hope and its fulfilment.
- The other is a more widespread context in the New Testament as a whole, and that is the great scandal of believing in a God who suffers. Why does he suffer? What does that achieve? What story can we tell that somehow connects that suffering with my life?

> ### Reflection
>
> As we conclude this section, think about these religious and social contexts and see if you can either a) see links between them and your own or b) find similar ways of describing the problems you face in both Christian belief and public Christian confession.

2

Worshipping Despite it All

1 Peter

Tracking down worship in New Testament texts is not as easy as you might think – and certainly not as straightforward as listing references to suffering. What is worship and how do we recognize it?

> **Reflection**
>
> You might like to think about this question from your own experience for a moment. How would you judge whether a piece of text contains worship material?

Here are some possibilities.

- We can define worship in very broad terms. One of my favourites is from a German scholar, Gerhard Delling:

  > Worship is the self portrayal of religion. In worship, the sources by which religion lives are made visible, its expectations and hopes are expressed and the forces which sustain it are made known.

  It's a great working definition but it doesn't help us a lot to identify worship in New Testament contexts.
- Or we can define worship in a much more narrow way, as related to liturgy, services and ceremonies. So we can look for snippets and extracts that look as if they might come from liturgical contexts. For example, in 1 Peter we might find hymns (e.g. 3.18–22 perhaps); creed-

like statements (like 2.22–4 maybe); a doxology (like the one at 5.11), a greeting that looks rather more formal than usual with references to Father, Son and Holy Spirit (1.2) and the reference to a holy kiss (the kiss of peace?) (5.14). The problem is that we can only judge these things by reference to much later works. In New Testament times there were no developed liturgies, and so we find ourselves reading back from liturgies a hundred or more years later, or even from our own experience today. There is so much ambiguous material here. What are we to make of the frequent references to the Old Testament? Is that part of a liturgical recital or just a passing reference to bolster a point? A further problem is: how short must an extract be for us to think it liturgical? What about the odd unusual word? At 1.6, 1.8 and 4.13 a word is used which, among the New Testament letters, is found only in 1 Peter, and which can be translated 'exuberant joy'. Is this perhaps a reference to some kind of worship experience?

- We can notice theological discussion that revolves around known worship occasions. 2.5 would be an example of theological description that includes the language of ceremonial acts:

  Like living stones be yourselves built into a spiritual house, to be a holy priesthood, to offer spiritual sacrifices acceptable to God through Jesus Christ.

- Most notable of all are the discussions around baptism; overtly at 3.21 and 22:

  Baptism . . . now saves you, not as a removal of dirt from the body but as an appeal to God for a clear conscience, through the resurrection of Jesus Christ, who has gone into heaven and is at the right hand of God, with angels, authorities, and powers subject to him.

but also, according to many scholars, in several other places by allusion (e.g. 1.22: 'having purified your souls by your obedience to the truth for a sincere love of the brethren . . .'). Fifty years ago there was even a lively debate around whether 1 Peter was actually a complete baptismal liturgy, like the ones later celebrated along with a eucharist at Easter.

> Exercise
>
> *Read 1 Peter chapter 1.* Decide for yourself what you would consider in this chapter to be 'worship material'. What criteria have you used? How subjective do you think your choice is? Has reading this chapter altered any of the criteria you set out above?

Actually, there's something rather exciting about reading these texts in this way. We are taken back to a time when this new Christian community is still working out what is distinctive about itself, and when the concepts in Delling's definition are still taking shape. Worship is a prior concept to liturgy, and here we are at the ground floor with a church that is aware in some ways of its newness and specialness, but has not yet reached the point where these can be given formal structure, at least in terms of an 'order of service'. In other words we see the stuff of worship without being able to say categorically that an act of worship is taking place.

Revelation

On the face of it, worship is easier to spot in Revelation. Here there are set-piece sequences of worship, usually taking place in heaven, that is, within the context of a vision. Chapters 4 and 5 describe heavenly worship both seen and heard, and chapter 19 is a full description of the marriage feast of the Lamb and its praise preliminaries. In between there are other hymns (such as 7.9–12, 11.15–18 and 12.10–12). There is the lament over Babylon in 18.1–17 which has a liturgical pedigree, together with a number of fragments of praise, doxologies and liturgical vocabulary, notably the word 'Amen', which occurs several times. Old Testament allusions and quotations abound in the book. The *Marana tha* prayer that occurs at 22.20 is found in later eucharist liturgies. Indeed, just as there was debate about 1 Peter's being a baptismal liturgy, at around the same time there was a debate around whether Revelation was a eucharistic liturgy. Scholars outlined ingenious schemes imagining how the sections of the book fitted sections of the service. This attempt to treat the vast amount of worship-like material with proper seriousness has not been generally accepted. It is the case, as the book itself tells us, that it is meant to be read in worship (1.3), and the thesis is an attempt to explore the implications of that. Nevertheless, in its detail, it is largely an argument from silence. For our purposes it is enough to note the material, to compare it with that in 1 Peter and to see if the criteria we used there fit here.

Exercise

Read Revelation chapters 4 and 5. These are reckoned to be liturgical theological declarations about creation and redemption respectively. What do you think about that? Do you see links between this material and any worship with which you are familiar?

In fact, at this point you might find it useful to read through the whole book, not trying to make sense of the science-fiction-like settings, but simply noting anything that fits your definition of worship. When your list is complete, consider how well distributed these references are, and how they seem to act as a kind of commentary, rather like a Greek chorus, on the rest of the action.

So how might it be possible to reflect on the connection between the suffering we've noted and the worship which seems to be such an important part of this developing theology?

One way might be to look at the three general headings for worship that we have noted in 1 Peter and Revelation, namely, Baptism, Eucharist and Praise, to see what kind of potential they offer as a means of reflecting on suffering. These examples are suggestive rather than exhaustive.

Baptism and suffering

Here are some possible leads to help us see essential links between baptism and suffering in these two books.

- Baptism, an act of entry to the Church, in so far as it is a communal act is presumably an act not just of initiation but of proclamation. This is a chance for the congregation to celebrate the theological truths it holds dear and which give it identity. These include beliefs about the saving work of Christ which makes baptism possible, the effects of the Spirit active in baptism, and the ultimate significance of the act in terms of the history of the world. Death and resurrection is a particular motif throughout the New Testament, though not, it must be said, in 1 Peter. Baptism is, in this sense, a public act of witness. In this connection it is interesting to note that both 1 Peter and Revelation use the Greek word *martus* (from which we get our word 'martyr'), meaning witness, more frequently than does, say, Paul.
- In Revelation there are several references to witnesses wearing white garments, a clear reference to baptism (3.4, 6.11, etc.), and while it would be assuming too much to equate baptism too closely with martyrdom, nevertheless there is a clear sense of the cost of discipleship, understood as witness.
- Witness in 1 Peter contains the two elements contained in 4.19 and 5.1, namely sharing Christ's sufferings and doing right. This doing right is the Christian's defence against opponents but may well lead to suffering. It may even be that the description of the author at 5.1 as 'a witness of the sufferings of Christ and partaker of his glory' means something equivalent to 'I have been baptized'. In a situation where the Church is vulnerable and threatened, baptism is very much 'standing up to be counted', in a way which will probably lead to suffering.
- In Revelation there is emphasis on the outward marks of belonging. In particular we see the idea of being sealed on the forehead as at 7.3 and 9.4. Here the seal is a mark of God's ownership and protection against the coming tribulation. It is that knowledge of ownership and protection that inspires witness.
- Not only baptism purifies. There is also the purifying action of fire – the baptism of fire if you like. The word that describes this occurs only three times in the New Testament, at 1 Peter 4.12 and Revelation 18.9 and 18.

> ### Exercise
>
> These are just a few possibilities. *Read Revelation chapter 7*, with the image of baptism in mind. If you had been recently baptized in Asia at this time, what would this say to you?

Eucharist and suffering

Links between eucharist and suffering are probably more familiar. New Testament writers clearly want us to make these connections as they link the eucharist to the Last Supper, in turn linked to Christ's passion. The Last Supper itself is a remembrance of the price of freedom from the suffering of slavery. The language of sacrifice is central to description of the eucharist. Attempts to understand the eucharist as a simple fellowship meal divorced from the context of suffering are quickly corrected (see for example the account of the journey to Emmaus, Luke 24.13–32, especially verse 5; also Paul's insistence that the eucharist is a proclamation of the Lord's death, 1 Corinthians 11, especially verse 26). Many scholars see the eucharist as a vehicle for reflecting on suffering, as well as being a way of demonstrating unity. In so far as the final feast in Revelation alludes to a eucharistic occasion it has as one purpose, the vindication of those who have endured the tribulation.

Praise and suffering

The songs of praise in Revelation include these themes.

- There is a strong affirmation of God's presence. Worship is both a recognition of God's presence and a means of making it real and effective. 7.10 and 12 is heavily influenced by imagery of the Jewish Feast of Tabernacles which celebrates, supremely, the joy of God's presence.
- Victory over evil is proclaimed in these songs. This is especially true from chapter 7 onwards when the great cry of 'salvation' is appropriate

and the great tribulation is over. The theme is replayed at 11.17 using imagery from Psalm 2. In some sense worshippers are allowed to participate in the victory.
- These songs also provide some continuity with the worship of Israel, and particularly the songs which come from the Exodus tradition celebrating victory over adversity.

> ### Exercise
>
> *Read Revelation 19.1–8:*
>
> > After this I heard what seemed to be the loud voice of a great multitude in heaven, crying,
> >> 'Hallelujah! Salvation and glory and power belong to our God, for his judgments are true and just;
> >> he has judged the great harlot who corrupted the earth with her fornication,
> >> and he has avenged on her the blood of his servants.'
> > Once more they cried,
> >> 'Hallelujah! The smoke from her goes up for ever and ever.'
> > And the twenty-four elders and the four living creatures fell down and worshipped God who is seated on the throne, saying, 'Amen! Hallelujah!' And from the throne came a voice crying,
> >> 'Praise our God, all you his servants,
> >> you who fear him, small and great.'
> > Then I heard what seemed to be the voice of a great multitude, like the sound of many waters and like the sound of mighty thunderpeals, crying,
> >> 'Hallelujah! For the Lord our God the Almighty reigns.
> >> Let us rejoice and exult and give him the glory,
> >> for the marriage of the Lamb has come,
> >> and his Bride has made herself ready;
> >> it was granted her to be clothed with fine linen, bright and pure' –
> > for the fine linen is the righteous deeds of the saints.
>
> This is the only occurrence of the word Hallelujah in the New Testament. The passage contrasts the whore and the bride. On the face of

> it (as if looking at grainy photographs taken with a long zoom lens) there are real similarities between a whore and a bride. What do you think are the differences for this writer? Does this help to define what Christians have to be, and what they have to avoid? Is there any link here with suffering?

In this section we have explored some ways of noticing worship in these two books, and have begun to think about how that worship might offer a suitable context for reflecting on suffering. In the final section we can ask, what did worship do for these suffering people, and can it do something for us that is in any way comparable?

3
Why Worship When You're Suffering?

For many people that might be the key question. In our culture we have come to associate worship so much with praise and thanks for how well things have gone, how many blessings we've received and how tremendously the crops have grown. At the first sign of trouble or disappointment, many people give up on church, claiming that their faith has been shattered. The idea that worship has a strong, even intrinsic link with suffering is rather novel to such people.

> ### Reflection
>
> Can you think of contexts where suffering and worship go hand in hand in modern society? Now read on and see if any of the links below help to illuminate those situations further.

From our brief exploration of 1 Peter and Revelation we might suggest that the following possibilities are worth considering as an answer to the question: What did worship actually do for these people?

1. Worship is a means of **consolation**. This is partly to do with the theme of **protection**. Baptism confers God's seal. The eucharist harks back to the Passover where those whose homes were marked out were protected. The idea of thereby being God's **possession** is consolatory. The epithets in 1 Peter 2.9 and 10 show how important this is. Being a **member of God's household** is important for the aliens and exiles. The

vindication motifs are also a means of consolation. No matter how things look now and how difficult it is to maintain purity and faith against the odds, we shall be vindicated in the end. This is stated more strongly in the final worship of Revelation than probably anywhere else in the whole New Testament. The context of prophecy and **fantasy**, which Revelation provides, with its ability to transport the hearer from a mundane world to a place of cosmic significance, also has a consolation function. The identification between the Christians' experiences of suffering and those of Christ himself, so important in 1 Peter, are to some extent conveyed both through baptism and eucharist. Finally the affirmation of **God's presence** is a consolation in a situation where part of the problem is his perceived absence.

2 Worship is a focus of **solidarity and unity**, both of which are particularly important in suffering contexts. In 1 Peter the spiritual home theme set out in 2.4–10 makes this explicit. The songs of praise of the vindicated in Revelation provide a strikingly dramatic kind of unity in worship. In the tradition, the eucharist has developed as a sign of unity, and both writers appeal to baptism as something their readers have in common. Credal statements, which nowadays feature in most liturgies, also have a prime function of stating common purpose and belief.

3 Worship is a means of establishing **identity**. The evidence from the correspondence with the emperor Trajan is that Christians were recognized by their worship, and that it was through a kind of ceremonial rite that they had opportunity to deny that identity. Baptism was a way of becoming a new kind of person – a constant theme in 1 Peter, which contrasts the present with the pre-baptismal past. Again the mark of belonging is a mark of possession and a badge of identity. All the material in 1 Peter relating to belonging is important here too.

4 Worship is a vehicle for both **polemic and apologetic**. Part of the way of establishing identity is to mark the difference between Christians and others. The polemic which commentators reckon to be directed towards both Jews and the emperor cult in Revelation, also has the effect of saying who we are. The very fact that Revelation is set on the Lord's day (Revelation 1.10) is one example. Emperors also had a Lord's day. Jews had a Sabbath. The Christian Lord's day was neither of these.

There is plenty of fierce polemic in Revelation; some of it, in chapter 18 for example, in a kind of liturgical frame. On the other hand worship can also proclaim what we do believe in a positive way. It can demonstrate the victory of Christ.

5 Hence worship is a place for doing theology. It offers a context for reflection and a place where experience can come face to face with tradition in a way which enables each to act upon the other.

> ### Exercise
>
> Consider this list of the functions of worship in a suffering community. How many do you recognize from your study? Are there others you might want to add? From your own experience of worship, are any of these functions important for it? What does this reflection tell you about the worship you have experienced?

This short study of 1 Peter and Revelation has been selective, but hopefully not frustratingly so. I would hope that as a result you have found these books more interesting; managed to make links between the situation they derive from and your own; found a means of reflection on how Christian discipleship today maintains a tradition of suffering, and how worship today fulfils functions of consolation, solidarity and identity. And whether the whole thing adds up to a way of doing theology that's worth thinking about. These books offer insights into questions which are crucial for members of any faith community today, and that's surely far more interesting than arguing about whether St Peter had a ghost writer.

> ### Final Exercise
>
> Look again at the list of questions and issues in the third paragraph of the introduction. Has this study brought you any nearer to answering them?

4

What to Do Next

To be absolutely honest, there is no one book, on either of these New Testament works, which picks up the thread from where we've left it. That leaves five options.

- Read a good commentary on 1 Peter.
- Read a good commentary on Revelation.
- Read a good book about worship in the New Testament, and its development in the earliest examples of Christian communities.
- Read a good book about suffering which might help stimulate reflection, or make links between the New Testament and the present.
- Read a more general introduction to the New Testament as a whole, or these non-Gospel, non-Pauline-letter bits of it, that summarizes some of the issues and introduces its own bibliography.

The commentary I usually recommend on 1 Peter, for its accessibility and fairness, is by M. E. Boring – an off-putting name but a good book. It's in the Abingdon series, published by Abingdon Press, Nashville (1999). The same author writes about Revelation and has a commentary in the Interpretation series published by John Knox Press, Louisville (1989). A slightly older commentary on Revelation is by John Sweet (Pelican Commentary, 1979 – not to be confused with the commentary on Revelation written early in the last century by W. B. Swete), which you could perhaps find in a good library; this really is an excellent introduction.

A local library may be able to get hold of a copy of Colin Hemer's book *The Letters to the Seven Churches of Asia in their Local Setting* (Eerdmans, 2001 in its latest edition), which will appeal to those with an interest in history or ancient geography especially. This book attempts to link the content of the letters to the seven churches with the actual features of the towns where the churches were situated. If you liked *The Da Vinci Code*, you'll love this. Otherwise L. L. Thompson's commentary, *Revelation*, also in the Abingdon series (1998), is a readable and fairly up-to-date introduction from a recognized scholar.

If you want to read about suffering start with Dorothee Sölle's book simply called *Suffering* (published by Fortress Press, Augsburg, 1975).

Good, accessible books on worship in the early Church are surprisingly difficult to come by. This is partly due to the fact that scholars are now much more reluctant than they once were to make assumptions about worship in this very early period. You might like to get hold of a copy of C. F. D. Moule's Grove booklet called *Worship in the New Testament* (1989) to begin to fill out the subject a little. General New Testament introductions which may fit the bill include Howard Marshall, Stephen Travis and Ian Paul, *Exploring the New Testament, Vol. 2: The Letters and Revelation* (SPCK, 2002). Works which summarize some current scholarship are Mark Allen Powell, *The New Testament Today* (Westminster John Knox, Louisville, 1999) and Philip B. Harner, *What are They Saying about the Catholic Epistles?* (Paulist Press, New York, 2004).

Of course you need do none of these but simply, having enjoyed this study, wait for the next Church Times Study Guide to appear.